T0129009

AUTOBIOGRAPHY
WRITING FOR SENIORS

AUTOBIOGRAPHY

WRITING FOR SENIORS

By

MARGOT A. TIRADO

Order this book online at www.trafford.com
or email orders@trafford.com

Most Trafford titles are also available at major online book retailers.

Printed in the United States of America.

ISBN: 978-1-4669-1093-5 (sc)
ISBN: 978-1-4669-1092-8 (e)

Trafford rev. 01/04/2012

 www.trafford.com

North America & International
toll-free: 1 888 232 4444 (USA & Canada)
phone: 250 383 6864 ◆ fax: 812 355 4082

CONTENTS

THINGS TO THINK
ABOUT BEFORE YOU START YOUR
AUTOBIOGRAPHY

NECESSARY / OPTIONAL MATERIALS

Loose leaf notebook

Three-ring binder

Paper—three ring

Large envelopes 8 1/2 x11 inches or larger

Accordion folder (optional: in place of large envelopes)

Pens, pencils, erasers

Tape 3recorder—optional

Video recorder—optional

Correction pen or tape

Large bound journal—optional

Scrapbook

TIPS FOR WRITING THE AUTOBIOGRAPY FOR SENIORS

Where to begin your autobiography

There is no one set way of writing your autobiography. It is your history done the way you feel led to do it. It does not have to be sequential (I was born . . .). You could begin with an interesting event in your life and branch off from there.

Finding a place to write or record

Select a quiet, comfortable place where you can set your memories free without the possibility of intrusion. Carry your recording device with you so as not to lose any precious thoughts.

Read an autobiography written by someone famous

One way to begin your work is to read the work of someone else such as Abraham Lincoln, Billy Graham, Steve Jobs or any of the many autobiographies on the market. Pay close attention to where they chose to begin their autobiography and what interesting way they started.

Who are you writing your autobiography for?

Before you put pen to paper, decide who you are writing your autobiography for. Is it for <u>you</u> to release some unresolved situations? Is it for <u>your children</u> so they will have a historical account of the family's legacy? Is it an account that pairs <u>historical data</u> with your own family's involvement in the shaping of history? Whatever the reason for writing, remember your purpose throughout the document.

Select a theme

Decide on an overall theme. Most autobiographies have an ongoing theme that reoccurs throughout the work. This tends to unify and make the story interesting.

Recalling things from the past

A number of things can serve as memory joggers; things that will help you recall some past event. One would be a review of family memorabilia. Look for family memorabilia such as photos, letters, documents (marriage licenses, birth certificates, military badges and honors,) pieces of clothing (wedding gowns, military uniforms, nurses uniforms, etc). Include these items in a large folder. For those items that are too large; take a picture, tag it, and include it in the folder. Reviewing these items can open a flood gate of memories.

Another method of jogging your memory is to return to an old, familiar place. Let the scenery take you back in time. Don't forget to record your feelings, sights, smells, and any other senses that come with the return to familiar places. Visit the old neighborhood, family house or plot, school, church, shopping center, doctor's office, city hall, etc.

If you can't take a trip back home, call someone from back in the day. Talk about the old days, share the memories, and make a point to keep in touch.

Go through the family recipe book, if you have one, and make one of the old favorite recipes. The aroma will probably take you back in time and brew up old memories. Scraps of paper with an old recipe could also do the trick.

In the Appendix you will find 25 activities that can serve as memory joggers to help you enter those forgotten memories that are waiting to be revived at the slightest nudge.

Selecting a cover for your autobiography

There are many beautiful journals that might suit your taste. Check your local stationary store or variety shop. Choose one that best depicts you and your style.

You may want to invest in something that reminds you of bygone times such as the old fashion black and white composition books that were used in school back in the day.

You may choose to design your own cover. Using a three-ring binder with clear outer plastic pocket you can make your cover totally YOU. Use a picture of yourself, a self-portrait, a self-caricature, a map, etc. Use anything that will portray who you are or what you love.

To type, hand write, or record your autobiography

If you are writing for someone else, please type or record your autobiography. Fancy handwriting styles, though beautiful, may be difficult for the reader. Using a clear, plain type is best for an autobiography that you plan to share.

You can hand write your autobiography and then have it typed or otherwise recorded. Ink tends to smear and fade over time. Pencil, although easiest to correct, is also easiest to erase. For the longevity of your document, I recommend typing and placing your typed pages in clear plastic sleeves designed to fit into a three-ring binder.

The other alternative would be audio or visual recording: making sure to save the stored information.

COURSE
AUTOBIOGRAPHY WRITING FOR SENIORS
INTROSPECTION

Introspection is the process of looking into oneself, through your own eyes, and determining who you are. The purpose of this autobiographical work is to help you see you and your influence on those around you. You will look at the good, some of the bad, and maybe some of the ugly.

You may not want to share the entire packet with your intended audience. It will be your decision to audit this work at your own discretion, depending on the purpose of your writing and with whom you intend to share this piece of work.

A major reason for writing your autobiography is to share with your children, grandchildren, great grandchildren, relatives, and friends how things used to be in your day and how you navigated the belief system and living situations of that time in history. This is the history of your life.

One reason to share the nitty-gritty of your life would be to help others understand what shaped you into the person you are. How you were raised and the how certain circumstances contributed to your life and influenced who you turned out to be.

Another reason for writing your autobiography could serve as a catalyst for unpacking years of heavy weights you've carried due to unforgiveness, isolation, anger, and/or unfaithfulness. In that case, this autobiography is for your benefit.

You will begin your inward look by answering the following questions as honestly as possible. Feel free to expand your answers, and above all, use your senses of hearing, sight, smell, taste, and feeling to relate your story. You may record your answers in writing, or on a video or auditory recording device. If using auditory or video, be sure to secure the information so that it will not be accidently erased.

IN YOUR EYES

1. Who are you; not just your name?
2. What are you really like?
3. What shaped you into who you are; what events, what treatment, what conditions?
4. Who had the greatest influence on you? Positive or negative? Explain.
5. Are you satisfied with who you are today?
6. What nickname would you give yourself?
7. How have you made a difference in the lives of others?
8. How have others made a difference in your life?
9. What do you see as being the major influence in your life that made you who you are?
10. If you could change one thing in your life, what would that be?
11. If you could make changes, beginning today, what would be the first thing you would do?
12. What would be the next thing you would do to change yourself today?
13. Do people really know you for who you are or do you mask your identity?
14. I am happy for—
15. I am disappointed that—

16. I am angry about—
17. I feel cheated because—
18. I have achieved—
19. I have failed—
20. I have hurt—
21. I feel hurt—
22. How can I change the disappointment, anger, and the feelings of being cheated and of being a failure?

For those things in my life I cannot change, I will—

For those people I have hurt in my lifetime, I—

For those people in my life I need to forgive, I—

For those people I have held grudges against, I—

> I wash the slate clean. I hold no grudges or animosity toward anyone. For those who may still be holding some feelings of hurt or resentment; I ask you to forgive me so that we both can be free.

Section A—Basic Background Beginning

Name

Who named you?

What does your name mean? (See activity #14 in Appendix)

Were you named after someone? (relative, historical character, radio, or TV character, or other?)

Do you have a nickname?

What is your nickname?

Who tagged you with that name?

Why?

Has your name ever been changed?

Place of birth (Place a small map of your birthplace in your memorabilia folder)

Date of birth (Include copy of your birth certificate, if possible. If not possible, explain why)

Ethnic Background

What country did your forefathers reside in?

What was your native language?

Do you speak any other language?

What is the language?

How did you learn the language?

Did your neighbors speak this language?

When did your family migrate to the United States? Why?

Where did your family first settle in the U. S.?

How long did your family remain there?

Parents

Mother: First, Middle, Maiden Name

Place of Birth (city, state, country)

Date of Birth

Education

Highest Grade Completed

Additional Training

Religious Persuasion

Raised by Parents?

Raised by other family member(s) (Name)?

Her parents' names (your grandparents names)

Mother

Place of Birth

Date of Birth

Raised by family member(s) other than parents?

Did you ever meet your mother's parents?

What do you remember about them?

What were you told about them?

Did you ever meet any <u>other of your mothers' relatives</u>?

What do you remember about them?
What were you told about them?

Father
    Place of Birth (city, state, country)
    Date of Birth
    Education
        Highest Grade Completed
        Additional Training
    Religious Persuasion
    Raised by Parents?
        Mother's name
            Date of Birth
            Place of Birth
        Father's name
            Date of Birth
            Place of Birth
    Raised by someone other than parents?

Did you ever meet <u>your father's parents</u>?
    What do you remember about them?
    What were you told about them?
Did you ever meet any of your father's relatives?
    What do you remember about them?
    What were you told about them?
Siblings
    Brothers/Sisters

Name(s)

DOB (Dates of Birth)

Older or younger than you

Special skills, traits, characteristics

What was your relationship with him/her during childhood?

How has your relationship change in adulthood?

Do you have any nieces or nephews from this sibling?

List their names.

Religious Background

What is <u>your</u> religious persuasion?

Are you actively following this religion?

Where do you attend church, temple, synagogue, mosque, other?

Is this the religious belief of your family?

If you changed religious beliefs since childhood, explain why.

What are some of the beliefs you live by?

Section B—Early Childhood Experiences

Infancy to age 4   Dates: _____-_____
>Preschool experience
>Babysitter
>Stayed at home with parent(s), grandparent(s), other relatives
>Did other relatives live with you?
>>Who were they and their relationship to you?
>>Your favorite food(s)?
>>Who cooked it?
>Family activities
>>Family activities you enjoyed most?
>House
>>Where? Describe
>>Describe the neighborhood
>>What did you like about the house?
>>What didn't you like about the house?
>>Memorable friends
>Family traditions
>Family vacations
>Celebrations

>How did your family celebrate holidays?
>>Christmas
>>Thanksgiving
>>New Years

       Easter

       4th of July

       Veterans Day

       Valentine's Day

       Other holidays

       Birthdays

Early Illnesses

Lasting Effects (if any)

Religious Training

Ages 5-8   Dates: _____-_____

 Grades:

  Education

   Name of School

   Location of School

   Walked, bussed, or driven to school

   Favorite Teacher(s)

   Memorable Friends

   Memorable Events

  Clubs/ Extracurricular activities

   Cub Scouts

   Girl Scout

   Drama

   Music

   Religious Training (after school)

   Memorable Event(s)

  Friends

  Special Neighbors

  Neighborhood Activities

  Specific Memorable Neighbor

  After school Activities

  Pet(s)

Ages 9-12   Dates: _____-_____

Grades:

Education:

Name of School

Location

Favorite Teacher(s)

Walked, bussed, driven to school

Memorable Friends

Memorable Events

Clubs/ extracurricular activities

Friends

Pets

Vacations with family, relatives, friends

Camp experience(s)

Religious experience

Family worship

Readings

Bible

Torah

Koran

Other

Special honors or recognition(s) received

Favorite thing(s) to do

How did you spend summer months?

Favorite animal(s)

TV shows or radio programs you enjoyed

Favorite actor, actress, singer, musician, sports figure

Who did you want to be like? Why?

Favorite Activities

    Movies

    Sports

    Art

    Music

    Other

How did you spend your weekends?

What did you usually do during the week?

Ages: 13-17   Dates: _____-_____
Grades:
  Education
      Name of School
      Location
      Walked, bussed, driven to school
      Favorite teacher(s)
      Memorable Friends
      Memorable Events
  Extracurricular Activities
  Friends
  Special Neighbor(s)
  Neighborhood Activities
  Memorable Neighbor(s) Why?
  After School Activities
  First Job
      Where?
      Doing what?
      Enjoyed? Didn't enjoy?
      How long did you work there?

  Second Job
      Where?
      Doing What?
      How long did you stay employed there?
      Why did you leave?

First Relationship
>   Name
>   Short details of relationship
>   How did it end?
>   Why?

Driving Experience
>   How old were you when you first started to drive?
>   How old were you when you got your first vehicle?
>   How old were you when you got your license?
>   >   What state?
>   >   Did you pass the driver's exam the first time?
>   >   What was your first vehicle?
>   >   >   How did you get it?
>   >   >   What happened to it?

>   How were your driving skills?
>   >   Did you have any accidents?
>   >   Tickets?
>   >   Driving Suspensions? Why?

Section C—Young Adult years

Ages: 17-21   Dates: _____-_____

Grades:

    Education

        Name of School

            Location

            Mode of travel

            College

            Trade School

            On-the-Job Training

                Career Choice

                Memorable Teacher, professor, leader

            Military

                Dates

                Branch

                Stationed

                Honors

                Battalion

                Wounded

                Special memories

                Current friendships from Military

            Special Friend(s)

        Memorable Event(s)

        Graduation

            Date

Degree
Certification
Dropped Out
    Why?
    What happened after that?

First career job
    Location
    Mode of Transportation
    Job Description
    Pay
    Residence
        With family
        With friends: Describe
        With relatives: Describe
        Alone: Describe
    Transportation

Section D—Adult Years

Ages: 21—

    Relationship(s)

        First

            Describe

    Marriage

        Date

        Honeymoon

            Location

            Describe

    First home together—location

        Children

            Names and genders

            Ages (in birth order)

            From previous relationship

        What drew you and your spouse together?

        Marriage difficulties

            How were they resolved?

    Family Times

        Location

        Family Worship and belief

        Family outings, vacations, activities

        Meals (together, different schedules)

        Discipline

            You, spouse, or together

Most memorable day

Saddest day

How did family spend down time?

     TV

     Board games

     Movies

     Other

     Dancing

     Music

     Outdoors

     Sports

     Camping

     Family pets

Most memorable moment

Overall family objective in life

Marriage Ended

     Why?

     Results

Re-marriage/relationship

     Name

     Location

     Children together

     Children from Previous Relationship

     What attracted you to your spouse?

     How has this marriage differed from the previous one?

How have you been affected by this marriage?
What are the difficulties you face(d)?
How are you trying to resolve them?
How are you performing differently than in the first?
What have you learned from the first marriage?
How are you trying to make this marriage work?

Section E—Retirement Years

Age: 65—current
Married

> How long have you been married?
>
> When is your anniversary?
>
> What do you love about your spouse?

Widowed

> How long have you been widowed?

Single

> How do you spend your day?
>
> What do you do on weekends?
>
> How do you spend the holidays?
>
> Are you enjoying life?
>
> What could you do to improve your life?
>
> > What is stopping you from doing it?
>
> People you visit
>
> People who visit you
>
> Activities you enjoy
>
> Places you go

Meals

> Do you cook?
>
> Where do you get your meals?
>
> Who prepares your meals?
>
> Who does your laundry?
>
> Who does the housework?

Currently, I feel

> *With this autobiography of my life, I hope to clear up any wrong I've done or any incorrect data that may have circulated about me. I also want to answer any questions that family or friends may have about what contributed to the way I am. Above everything, I want you to know that I love you.*

YOUR LIFE IN RETROSPECT

As we age, many of us spend time looking back on our spent lives; how things could have been different, and why they weren't different. We all would be wiser if we could live our lives in retrospect, but we must take things a day at a time as they are presented to us. There is a purpose for looking back, however, and that is to avoid making the same mistakes again.

What would you change about you to make your family's life better?

What would you NOT want to change about you?

What is the greatest legacy, you feel, you have to leave to your family, friends, and society via this autobiography?

APPENDIX

ACTIVITIES
AUTOBIOGRAPHY WRITING FOR SENIORS

1. Go back to your childhood home, place of birth, or early neighborhood. Take a camera and take pictures of your old house, plot, church, school(s), main streets, doctor's office, drug store, restaurants, court house, playground, etc. Use these pictures to contrast then and now.

2. On your journey back home, stop in on some of the old addresses. Maybe you will find some of your fellow members of that day and time or perhaps you can locate someone who remembers you and your family. Spend time reminiscing. Get their phone numbers and addresses to keep in touch or just to say thank you for spending time with you. Don't forget to take notes or record your conversations.

3. If you cannot travel back to your homeland, use the computer to look up the area you grew up in and try to remember things that happened in certain areas and people who were there as mayor, physician, postal service workers, grocery store keeper, movie

receptionist, news reporters, teachers, principals, police officers, firefighters, etc. at that time.

4. Using an ink pad, make a copy of your fingerprints by placing your four fingers and thumb on the ink pad then onto a clean sheet of paper. Press firmly, trying not to smudge. Lift your hand carefully off the paper and clean the ink off your hand with soap and water or a wet wipe.

5. When your finger prints are thoroughly dry, place your hand directly over the prints and trace your entire hand print. In the empty hand space, write; "With these hands I have . . . ." Fill out some of the things you have done with your hands such as changed diapers, cooked dinner, bathed my baby, chopped wood, etc.

6. What outstanding event(s) or people have changed the course of your life forever?

7. Dedicate a section of this work to: What was going on at the time of my birth and during my childhood? Include the dates from birth to young adulthood. Describe the style of clothing being worn, prominent events, ruling government parties in office, wars, events within your family and neighborhood, etc.

8. Include a map of the place(s) and dates where you grew up. Indicate some of the prominent places such as school, hospital, police station, court house, park, playgrounds that you visited.

9. Include a map showing the different places where you lived. Trace a line noting the dates when you lived in that location, when and where you moved next. Continue the trace to current times if possible.

10. Insert a section of <u>MY FAVORITES</u> in your folder.

11. List your favorite. Explain why.

        Type of vehicle
        Season(s)
        Day(s) of the week
        Political party
        President
        Teacher(s)
        Color(s)
        Animal(s)
        Food(s)
        Time(s) of day
        Kind of shoes
        Sport
        Pet
        Newspaper(s)

Magazine(s)

MY FAVORITE

Shirt/blouse	Musician(s)
Painter(s)	Skirt/pants
Past time	Actress(es)
Hobby	Actor(s)
Person	Movie(s)
Brand of cigarette	TV show(s)
Brand of tobacco	Meat(s)
Comedian(s)	Vegetable(s)
News caster(s)	Fruit(s)
Singer(s)	Drink
Song(s)	Piece(s) of furniture
Dance(s)	Poem(s)
Place(s)	Writer(s)
Radio program(s)	Book(s)
Games	Ways to entertain yourself
Toys	

12. Write your own Obituary. Include how you would want to be remembered. Read some of the obituaries listed in your newspaper to see the kinds of information included.

13. If you could live anywhere, where would it be and why?

14. Search the origin and meaning of your name. Go to the library or online.

15. Research who was in political office in your locale at the time of your birth and during your early childhood years. Include a copy in your memorabilia folder.

16. Write the words to your favorite song as you sing it.

17. Write a poem about writing your autobiography or memoirs.

18. Include a copy of your favorite poem.
19. Complete the following table

Looking back	Stepping back	Reconnect?
Style of clothes worn	How did they look?	Y/N
Music then	How did it sound	Y/N
	How did it make you feel	
Theatre	What thoughts did it create	Y/N
Sports	What sports did you play	
	What sports did you enjoy watching	
Education	Was it worthwhile	Y/N

Friendships	Worthwhile	Y/N
	Lasting	Y/N
Family relationships	Close or distant	
Early Residence	Memorable, horrible	
Economic times	good, poor, barely survived	
Religious upbringing	valuable, inconsistent, none	

20.   <u>SENSORY ASSOCIATIONS</u>

What do you think of when you	
<u>SMELL</u>	Write-
<u>SEE</u> a rose	
<u>TOUCH</u>	
What do you think of when you	
<u>HEAR</u>	the phone ring late at night
	Write-
What do you think of when you	
<u>TASTE</u>	hot coffee in the morning
<u>SMELL</u>	Write-
How do you feel when you	
<u>SEE</u>	a young child crying
	Write-
<u>HEAR</u>	
What do you do when you	
<u>SEE</u>	someone homeless
	Write-

What do you do when you

HEAR	an accident
SEE	Write-

What do you say when someone asks you for money
Write-

21.   MORE SENSORY ASSOCIATIONS

What do you REMEMBER when you SEE a:

Rainbow

Large body of water

Kitten

Baby

Dilapidated house

Tiny house

Beautiful car

Child being abused

Pony

Funeral home

What do you REMEMBER when you HEAR a:

Fire engine

Smoke alarm

School bell

Alarm clock goes off
People running and yelling
Gunshots
Crying
Sneezing
Difficulty breathing
Chocking

What do you REMEMBER when you SMELL

Smoke
Apple pie
Chicken cooking
Urine
Perfume/cologne
Gasoline
Wood burning
Bread baking
Mountain air

What do you REMEMBER when you FEEL /TOUCH

Warm, wet skin
Shoes too tight
Fluffy slippers
Wet hair
Towel

Comfy chair or sofa
Silk nighty
Beach sand
Grungy sheets
Snowy weather

What do you REMEMBER when you <u>TASTE</u>

Hot apple pie
Pork chops
Turkey
Ice cream
Oatmeal
BBQ
Spinach
Watermelon
String beans

22. Interview relatives and friends from the past. Share your memories. You'll probably recall some things you had forgotten.

23. Visit a nearby nursing home. The residents would love to engage you in talk about days gone by. You may have some memories in common.

24. Read at least one autobiography. Notice how it begins? Where in the life journey did the author begin?

25. Sit near a large body of water and let the threads of your memory freely roam. Record what you see, feel, taste, hear and how those sensory devices open your memory to past events and feelings.

KEYS TO UNLOCKING YOUR MEMORY BANK

A. Old pictures—
    Pictures of bygone times can create a review of your
    memory cells.

B. Old letters and notes—
    Letters and notes can revive one's spirit and fuel
    one's memory.

C. Vacation memorabilia—
    Flyers, magazines, announcements, payment stubs,
    rental receipts, pennants, post cards, stamped
    napkins, stamped gift items can bring your memories
    out of hiding.

D. Clothing styles—Try to locate an old clothing catalog
    to view "back in the day" styles or old photos to bring the
    styles back to mind.

E. Era research—
    Check out old news clippings, historical society
    records, libraries for information about what was
    happening during your day in that specific locale or
    country.

F. Search areas of your house where you store things
    such as the attic or basement.

Pull out the old, stashed away pieces. The smell and the feel will probably open a floodgate of memories.

G. Other places to look—

> Internet
>
> Maps
>
> Newspaper Archives
>
> Catalogs
>
> Clothing, machinery, shoes
>
> Court House Records—
>
> Vital Statistics
>
> People—
>
> Trips to the hometown of your youth—
>
>> Your memory can get a huge nudge when you return to your old hometown where you grew up. Perhaps not all of the buildings or sites have been preserved but some will still be there. Imagine where things used to be.
>
> Visit your old—
>
>> School
>>
>> Church
>>
>> Hospital
>>
>> Doctor's office
>>
>> Cemetery
>>
>> Newspaper office
>>
>> Court House
>>
>> Neighborhood

Beach
Boardwalk
Neighbors
Factory

Sports arena or building
Playground

AUTOBIOGRAPHY WRITING FOR SENIORS

Timeline

Name: _____

      First   Middle   Last

Nickname _____

Nationality or Origin _____

Meaning of your name (see Appendix #14)

_____

CHILDHOOD	YOUNG ADULT YEARS
Enter dates: Birth to Early Childhood Age: Infant—4	Enter dates: Ages: 17-25

EARLY CHILDHOOD	ADULT YEARS
Enter dates: Ages: 4-8	Enter dates: Ages: 26-65

MIDDLE CHILDHOOD	RETIREMENT YEARS
Enter dates: Ages: 9-12	Enter dates: Ages: 65+

TEEN YEARS

Enter Dates:	Enter current date:
Ages: 13-17	Enter current age:
	Signature _____

B   M   R

1. Beginning at B, write in the year of your birth.
2. At M (mid-point), write the year that indicates your middle year.
3. At R, write the year you turned 65.
4. Fill in pertinent dates along the timeline. If necessary, increase the line.

GET THE FACTS

Interview:

Relatives—Thrash out dates, conditions, names, locations, conversations, and any other information that will clarify data from the past.

Friends—Talk with old friends who knew you when you were younger. Share memories.

Search legal documents and records.

Search news clippings in the newspaper archives.

AUTOBIOGRAPHIES BY FAMOUS PEOPLE

Here is a brief, non-conclusive list of published autobiographies that you may be interested in reading. Check with your librarian for others.

Angelou, Maya. "I Know Why the Caged Bird Sings."

Berle, Milton. "Milton Berle. An Autobiography."

Frank, Anne. "The Diary of A Young Girl."

Jefferson, Thomas. "The Autobiography of Thomas Jefferson."

Keller, Helen. "The Story of My Life."

Kipling, Rudyard. "Something of Myself."

Linkletter, Art. "I Didn't Do It Alone."

Meir, Golda. "My Life."

Quinn, Anthony. "The Original Sin. A Self Portrait."

MEMORABILIA

You may select to add any of the following or other items to your Memorabilia folder.

maps	receipts	photos	bills
notes	journals	schedules	Bible
voter registry	diaries	letters	diagrams
flyers	death certificates	deeds	cards
report cards	licenses	hospital records	passports
wills	invitations	year book	library cards
town records	college transcripts	immigration papers	obituaries
military records	real estate records	city hall records	scrap books
news clippings	chamber of commerce	birth certificates	headstones
Bible records	baptismal records	church records	
home movies	naturalization papers	divorce decrees	

RENOWNED FAMILY MEMBERS AND FRIENDS

Who do you know that is (was) famous?

Were you on friendly, speaking terms with them?

Where and when did you meet or were told about them?

How did they treat you?

How did you feel about them?

Did you ever visit them at their house? What was the house like? Describe.

Do you have any pictures that were taken with them?

When was the last time you saw or talked with them?

Are you still in touch with them or their children?

THE END

Printed in the United States
By Bookmasters